THE AMERICAN EAGLE

THE AMERICAN EAGLE

Photographers
TOM AND PAT LEESON

Editor
CYNTHIA BLACK

Designer
DOROTHY JANE WIEDEN

BEYOND
WORDS
Publishing
INC

The EARTHSONG Collection

Beyond Words Publishing, Inc.
4443 NE Airport Road
Hillsboro, OR 97124
Phone: 503-693-8700
Toll Free: 800-284-9673

Distributed to the book trade by Publishers Group West.
Printed in the United States of America.

Printed by Dynagraphics, Inc., Portland, Oregon
Separations by Wy'East Color, Portland, Oregon

ISBN: 0-941831-30-2 Hard Cover
ISBN: 1-895270-08-1 Soft Cover
Library of Congress Catalog Card Number: 88-71833

Other books in the EarthSong Collection

Migrations

Wisdomkeepers

Light on the Land

Within a Rainbowed Sea

Quiet Pride

A Circle of Nations

Keepers of the Spirit

Moloka'i—An Island In Time

The corporate mission of Beyond Words Publishing, Inc.

Inspire to Integrity

The corporate values

We give to all of life as life has given us

We honor all relationships

Trust and stewardship are integral to fulfilling dreams

Collaboration is essential to create miracles

Creativity and aesthetics nourish the soul

Unlimited thinking is fundamental

Living your passion is vital

Joy and humor open our hearts to growth

It is important to remind ourselves of love

*To our parents,
whose love has enabled
our lives and our work.*

I am the eagle
I live in high country
in rocky cathedrals
that reach to the sky

And all those who see me
and all who believe in me
share in the freedom
I feel when I fly

Come dance with the west wind
and touch all the mountain tops
sail o'er the canyons
and up to the stars
and reach for the heavens
and hope for the future
and all that we can be
and not what we are

John Denver
"The Eagle and the Hawk"

Through space and time
The American Eagle carries
the reader to certain enchanted places:
places which have a potent magic in them.
It is a magic compounded of many
elements: sunshine, blue sky, trees,
leaves, and clouds; silences, fragrances,
sweeps of distance; colors, shadows,
numberless shapes of life; bird voices,
the flight of eagles across the sky, the
symmetry of deer; these and many
other things, small and tremendous,
tangible and intangible, some of
them perceived with the senses,
others dreamed of
and vividly imagined.

In soul and essence this is a book
about the beauty of eagles — their
beauty as we see them alive and free
in green places where they are at home.
The utmost that can be hoped for
is that it may help in some small
measure to bring nearer the day when
man shall cease to be a destroyer and
shall become instead the friend
and protector of his lesser kinsmen —
the guardian and preserver of that
marvelous life of earth and air over
which, in the course of long
ages, he has achieved
absolute power.

Herbert Sass

I watched a pair of eagles
building a nest one winter dawn in the skeleton of
a pine. While first light eased back the darkness, ghosts of my
people formed and mingled with the morning mist beneath the
lifeless tree. For the ghosts are of the land, and can manifest in
times of need. The arrival of two eagles explains all this. The
dead pine they selected was rooted in a nature park overlooking
a brackish, freshwater lake. All around, the land here yields
artifacts of broken and scattered people who once soared in
spirit to the heights eagles inspired.

White Deer of Autumn

Some natural objects are so profoundly moving that they have a species of visual poetry about them. They sing of glory and wonder. I am moved this way by snow-capped mountains, pacing pumas and the great aerialists among our eagles. Such spectacles are impressive mainly because they overwhelm the eye. They may do this with color, glorious movements, shape, symmetry, texture, and even their setting. Their impact is overwhelmingly visual; we primates share with all birds the feature of being vision-dominated to an extreme. From this may spring our artistic sensibilities. A Breughel or a Gauguin has magic for me, touching common chords with the beauty of the living planet. It is therefore totally appropriate that a book that is exclusively devoted to the bald eagle should be so extensively pictorial. A bird so aesthetically pleasing and so intrinsically beautiful deserves to be celebrated in pictures, and what pictures these are! The photographs in this volume raise technical expertise to the level of artistry that is found in masterworks.

One of my favorites is of a simple feather that the photographer's eye transforms into an exquisite piece of filigree. Not that feathers are really simple. As an extraordinary end product of an extended period of evolution, the feather is worth consideration in addition to the superb photography. The feather is the essence, the very quiddity of what makes a bird a bird. The feather's fine structure of barbs, cross-linked by finer barbules, is an intricate solution to a difficult mechanical problem. The crotchets and hooks of the inter-linking barbules resemble Velcro tape in permitting the aerodynamic surface to be separated and then rejoined. The end result is something that combines lightness, deformability, and strength in a unique and complex way. The feather's vanes can be disturbed and displaced by the trauma of aerobatics and then restored by the act of preening. The complementarity of feathers and preening is essential to the flight of birds, from the magnificence of soaring to the astounding maneuverability of hummingbird hovering. The structure is beauteous, and preening has an intimate fascination in its overwhelming sensuality.

And feathers are not for flight alone. Contour feathers give the eagle or the sparrow its energy-efficient low drag streamlining, and down feathers insulate the hotter-than-mammals body temperatures of birds. Downiness is an appropriate adjective. As if the intrinsic beauty of the beast were not enough, in these pictures it is many times set against a backdrop of wild scenery that for once merits the expletive "breathtaking." Much of the scenic grandeur of America is contained in this book alongside the portraiture of our national bird.

Enough of words about what the eye can decide! What about the bald eagle itself? Here is a bird, chosen as a national symbol, which has so many features that seem appropriate to epitomize national aspirations and characteristics. The head is strikingly proportioned with character, the eyes announce vigilance, and the powerful curved beak seems hewn of steel. The widespread wings project an image of overwhelming stability and strength. Additionally as a fishing eagle it exercises massive surveillance over the sea-girt edges of the nation and ranges widely over inland waters. It was surely a good choice. Of course any piece of symbolism finds detractors. In this case some critics point at the bald eagle's occasional scavenging as though this somehow demeans its status. No biologist would thus argue, nor would one apply moral overtones to this role.

There is no question that predator/scavengers play an entirely disproportionately important role in relation to their numbers in maintaining the health and balance of living systems. They are the regulators of numbers and the cleansers necessary for the maintenance of nature's energy cycles. Without them nothing would work. Cast in this light the symbolism acquires broader and more general significance. There is no doubt that our world at this moment is in dire need of cleansing and replenishing. It is worth a passing mention that the National Zoo chose for its logo a bald eagle mother tending her chick. This image at one and the same time celebrated our success in breeding the species and our zoo's national character. In addition it projected the image of care and loving protection for the helpless that characterizes the conservation function of zoos.

American Indian attitudes toward the bald eagle are represented in this volume by poetry and lyrical prose. Nothing could be more appropriate. The bald eagle figures prominently in the history and culture of the First Americans. To return to feathers once more, the eagle feather was part of their ritual and magic. It marked the warrior as a badge of courage; to wear it he had to earn it by killing an enemy in battle. Later in history, it came to pass that the feather was awarded not for killing but for ritually vanquishing a foe by counting coup on him. Surely this is one of the most ecologically sound ways of solving disputes.

From now on we can only hope that our eagle will sustain all of us as we pause at the edge of the twenty-first century. Such beauty, grace and majesty, revealed gloriously in this book, should never be allowed to perish from the land, but must be encouraged to spread and multiply like the hope of freedom that it now symbolizes.

Michael H. Robinson
Director, National Zoological Park

As I watched the great birds
wheeling in the dawn, thoughts floated
in my mind like sacred feathers falling,
and I reached out to grasp them.
Eagle feathers are the intercessors of prayer,
healers of life, evocations of memory.
The one I held in my mind at that
moment helped me recall the births
of my children.
I could remember fanning my
wife with eagle feathers while she
labored, cooling her with strong,
magical breezes;
and the feathers brushed
the soft cheeks
of each newborn's face at birth and
brought them their first breaths.

I watched
the white-headed eagles then,
as they circled over the sunpools
and shadows
of this remaining sanctuary,
circling in their own
anticipation of birth.

With their black wings spanning
greater than the height of
most men, they lifted and guided
themselves into the blue air
while their white tail feathers
glistened
in the light of an unseen sun.

During that time
of wonder and reflection,
the ghosts shimmered away
in the settling mists
until I alone remained,
watching the eagles
spiraling down
again
and again,
clutching in their talons
the sedge and sticks
to make their place
of newness
out of something old.

I saw circles within circles,
the way all things flow,
including what I know.
Is this the kind of thing
ancestral eagle watchers
once observed
and thus inspired?

White Deer of Autumn

The eagle's home, in soft lofty treetop, is a castle indeed. It is built of sticks, some of them five feet or more in length and almost as thick as a man's wrist, sod, weeds, grass, moss, bark, pinetops, stalks, and branches of various kinds.

The eagles, which are believed to be mated for life and which probably live to a great age if no accident befalls them, return to the same nest year after year, adding new material to the structure each season, so that ultimately it attains an immense size.

Nests six or seven feet in height and six feet wide are not uncommon, and there is a record of one nest, occupied for at least thirty-four years, which is twelve feet tall and eight and a half feet wide across the top. In a shallow depression at the top of the nest the female deposits two, occasionally three, great white eggs.

There is no spectacle in the whole world of birds so inspiring as the soaring eagle floating on outstretched wings in "those blue tracts above the thunder" which are his true home and kingdom.

Something of the grandeur of that spectacle is due to association, to the great part which the eagle has played in history, and to the almost supernatural powers attributed to him in legend and myth. But it is not wholly this aura of tradition that invests the eagle, whenever seen, with an interest more compelling and more nearly universal than that inspired by any other feathered creature. He is in his own right a bird of unsurpassed power and majesty, the finest and strongest of the great order of martial birds, the *Raptores* or birds of prey, which include in their number the swiftest and most formidable of the denizens of the air.

The eagle is among birds what the lion is among beasts; and in many ways his appeal to the imagination is even stronger than that of the lion, due largely to his habit of soaring to magnificent heights, to his superb and commanding aspect when standing at rest, and to the spectacular and imposing nature of his aerial evolutions when seeking and pursuing his prey.

Herbert Sass

From the earliest times, the eagle, in one form or another, has played an important part not only in literature but also in the history of nations. His great size, his swiftness and strength, his noble and fearless aspect, the majesty of his flight when sweeping onward across the heavens, and the splendid and terrible power of his onset — all these things, appealing equally to the poet and the soldier, distinguished him among all the other inhabitants of the air and revealed him, through a mist of legend which magnified his powers, as the very archetype of invincible valor, the incarnation of all the most admired attributes of the warrior.

Thus, by a natural process, the eagle became a symbol, even a deity of war. The Persians bore him forward into battle upon their spears; he was the emblem of the kings of Babylon and of ancient Egypt; the Romans hailed him not only as the Bird of Jove but also as the Bird of Rome, and the sight of him in the sky on the eve of conflict was almost an assurance of triumph. Marius declared him exclusively the standard of the Roman legion; no lesser unit of the Roman army was deemed worthy of the imperial bird. Charlemagne, combining under his rule the Latin and German empires, adopted the double-headed eagle as the fitting emblem of his sovereignty; and in diverse forms and under many banners the eagles of Rome and of Charlemagne have flown in the dust of countless battlefields through all the centuries that have followed. To the armies of Prussia, of Czarist Russia, of Hapsburg Austria, and of Napoleonic France the eagle was the bird of war, the personification of all the virile virtues of the soldier, the perfect symbol of victory.

All this — exaggerated and half-mythical though it may be — is part of the eagle as we see him today in life; and all this, all that he has symbolized in the rise and fall of empires, in the crash of contending armies, in "dust of battle and deaths of kings," is one reason why it is difficult to write about the bird himself, the eagle of flesh and blood, without in some measure glorifying him. The eagle, "soaring above earth's clouds and seeking the sun in the heavens," has become a legend, an image in the mind. He belongs as much to literature as to natural history, and we never see him without being affected, unconsciously perhaps, by the glamour that tradition has spread around him.

He is a king in truth, this snowy-headed ruler of the sky-spaces; a king in the older and better sense in which kingliness meant strength, courage, nobility of bearing. Broad-shouldered, compact, powerfully muscled, massive yet clean of build, he is the peer in stalwart beauty of any of his royal race. His trenchant talons, his great hooked beak are weapons of deadly power. His wide dark pinions, of ample spread, can drive him at impressive speed through the air or lift him high above the earth to dizzy altitudes. At rest or on the wing, in repose or in action, he is a worthy member of that storied race of birds which, in all ages and in many countries, has stirred more deeply than any other the imagination of mankind.

Herbert Sass

Above convention's ribbon-narrow roadway, the eagle plays with gravity, with light.

In the open airs of sunspun clouds and moonlit nights she flies, her wings unfurled. Trees dwindle, fall away, until beneath her is only a rolling green forest, horizon to horizon, lakes like eyes, rivers snaking toward the sun.

To feel as the eagle feels! To know wind as the eagle knows wind! To breathe as the eagle breathes, to see as she sees, to glide with her, to ride with her upon the drafts, spiraling higher, ever higher, looking for her mate.

Is that him above the distant canyon now? A mere dot at first, playing with the winds? Is he perchance looking also for her?

And then with eyes that on a clear day could see her a hundred miles away, he finds her in the sky and turns to fly in her direction.

"Calawa, alawa, talawa, clamoy," he cries!

"Clamoy! Awala, awala, hoiya hoie!" she replies, sailing toward him through the heavens.

As their bodies coast the last wingbeat toward union, their feathers cup, catch the wind in celebration, in prayer. And there in the sea-blue open air, their bodies join. Mating, they unite — great feathered wings embracing, warm bodies in the sky. United, they tumble, falling free. Gravity yields, gives way. Weightless they float in ecstasy. Coupled. Suspended for a moment out of time.

Just before they hit the treetops, the plummeting eagles will separate in symmetrical arcs and curve upward, wings spread once more to fly side by side to the nest in some craggy peak where the eggs will be placed and cared for.
But that time is not yet.

Now. Together. They fall.
And now, while gravity is suspended,
the baby eagle is conceived,
created in the air,
in a weightless realm
between the worlds.

Ken Carey

The eagle soaring against the sky
seems free. As free as the clouds, the
winds, the fog drifting across the lake. In reality
the eagle is not free at all, except perhaps
when young and not yet anchored to
mate or nest site. For the rest of its life,
if it succeeds in entering the breeding
population, the eagle lives in bondage,
not to the mate, but to the master of both,
the territory and particularly the giant
nest to which it has become a lifelong
caretaker. Wherever the eagle travels,
its home territory exerts a magnetic force
drawing it back. The eagle's freedoms
become little freedoms. It may choose
the perch on which it rests, the food it
pursues, the hour when it hunts, but it
does not escape the demands of the nest.
The choice is not its own.

George Laycock

P laning from sky to sky on cushions of thermals
as though powered foils,
these six by six or seven by seven foot feathered airships
navigate in awe-inspiring glory along ridge or waterway
as they migrate from north to south and south to north
with the rhythm of the seasons.

Stanwyn G. Shetler

Oₙ their breeding grounds or even in migration
when there is a surfeit of thermals,
they often soar upward in ever-widening spirals
until, as mere specks against the azure heavens,
they suddenly vanish, escaping through the roof of the sky.

Stanwyn G. Shetler

A newly hatched eaglet
        is a weak and feeble little creature
    that cannot raise its heavy head
on its rather thin neck, cannot see properly
        through partly closed eyes, and must be
    continuously brooded by its parent.

It may not take any nourishment for twenty-four
to forty-eight hours after hatching, and when it does
    it must be very carefully
    and gently induced
    to feed by the powerful parent.
  The parent tears off shreds of red flesh
    from prey and holds them out to the eaglet
on the tip of the hooked bill.
    The eaglet, which like other birds of prey
    is inclined to peck at anything red,
    pecks at the flesh
    and so takes its first small meal.
        If the eaglet cannot be induced to feed
            it will die;
        it cannot be force-fed
                by the parent.

Leslie Brown

The eagle,
like all the other big birds of prey, is often annoyed by crows
and by smaller birds of various kinds which know
that they are comparatively safe because of their small size
and superior agility.

Herbert Sass

Man's reverence for these regal birds of prey
dates back to earliest human history.
Primitive man, staring into the skies,
marveled at the giant birds whose mysterious powers
let them soar to the limits of human vision and beyond.
They sailed the skies with a sense of freedom
that, in the minds of the ancients, bridged the chasm
between the world of man
and the land of the spirits.

George Laycock

The air has become one vast highway for man
riding in his aircraft,
but we must remember that it has always been a skyroad
for the eagle and any other flying bird.
It is the travelway over which birds can move
to any place on earth; a haven from their enemies of the ground;
a source of all their companions.
It is a realm of all the storms that affect birds;
a place where they can gather food by day;
a world of moonlight and stars
that light their night migrations.

John K. Terres

A "white-headed sea eagle," as its Latin scientific name translates, is the bald eagle that inhabits coasts, shores of lakes and rivers. The eagle makes its living from the water, eating principally fish, and never strays far from shore except sometimes during migration.

Stanwyn G. Shetler

$\underline{\hspace{1cm}}$ No one had to tell me
that the two eagles I watched throughout
the winter were gone one day last spring.

I felt the loss already,
and the anguish of knowing
what dangers awaited them on their flyway north
churned my stomach.

Now, there is only their empty nest
atop a skeleton of the Tree of Peace,
but the ghosts may still be summoned
among the spirit of dead leaves next autumn,
to wait quietly in the cool morning mists with me. ▤

White Deer of Autumn

The first feathers of the juvenile are dark brown, almost black, and they are worn through the remainder of the bird's first year. Bald eagles undergo one molt annually, beginning in spring and proceeding gradually through early autumn. In succeeding years white begins to appear on the head and tail, mixed at first with the dark brown, until in the fully adult state — in the eagle's fifth or sixth year — the dark chocolate brown contrasts sharply with the gleaming white of the head and tail.

George Laycock

In his appeal to the finer faculties of the mind,
the eagle soars far above biological actuality,
lifted on high by a mightier power
than that of his own great wing —
the immeasurable glamor of all that he has symbolized
in the legend, the history, the poetry of the past.

Herbert Sass

The eagle has always been a favorite heroic image in literature and song, as in the metaphorical imagery of biblical writers to whom the eagle (though they did not know the bald eagle) is a symbol of exalted status, youthful strength, swiftness, farsighted vision, fierceness, freedom from earthly ties, and above all, God's care for his children.

Thus, Isaiah writes, "But they that wait upon the Lord shall renew their strength; they shall mount up with wings as eagles . . . ."

Stanwyn G. Shetler

The eagle is even more familiar
as an element of the Golden Age of Greece
and within the might of the Roman Empire.
In Grecian mythology, the eagle
was portrayed as the emblem of Zeus,
ruler of the heavens, father of other gods
and of mortal heroes.
An eagle always attended the capricious
king of Olympus and served as his messenger.
It was the only bird that dwelt in heaven.
Impervious to lightning, the eagle was able
to grasp Zeus' wrathful thunderbolts.
The eagle stole Ganymede from earth
for Zeus' pleasure and was immortalized
in the northern sky as Aquila,
the eagle stars, for that service.

Gay Monteverde

The life of the nest
may span decades.
If an eagle's mate dies,
the survivor, still tied to the home territory,
is driven to travel
beyond the distant hills,
rivers, and lakes,
searching for a new mate.

The old nest becomes, in turn, master
of the latest arrival. Then, if its mate should die,
it may in turn depart in search of a mate and,
with good fortune, bring another strange eagle
to share the nest which neither of them built
but both will repair, maintain, and use
as long as they or the nest remains.

In this way the eagle's nest
spans generations. Such was the rule
of the eagle's world when the birds
had only to contend with natural forces,
and before man began disrupting the pattern,
destroying the trees, disturbing the birds
by crowding into their wilderness,
or killing them outright.

George Laycock

The eaglet passes his novitiate so slowly
        that at the age of four weeks parts of the
        plumage are present, the second down
        coat still bearing relics of the natal down
        which precedes it and traces
            of the developing juvenile
        feathers which follow.

            The beautiful hackle feathers
        of the neck develop so slowly in
        comparison with those of other parts
    that when the eaglet has attained his
    sixth week, he has no cause to be proud
        of his appearance. From this time on,
        however, the young eagle slowly
        acquires his handsome juvenile dress,
        changing from dark umber to raven
        black on wings and tail and shining like
        a new silk hat.

By the time he is ready for independent flight
        he is a swarthy giant,
            as large as or larger than his parents;
            he has a dark bill, hazel eyes,
                sports yellow "boots,"
            and carries a formidable set of talons
            which are now mainly black.

Francis Hobart Herrick

A distant
white spot
on the water
determines
the bird's course.
It descends swiftly
to the target,
dips one talon
into the water,
clasps the fish,
and carries it off
toward the eyrie
without pause. ▪

George Laycock

CLASS: *Aves,* which includes all birds.

ORDER: *Falconiformes,* which includes most diurnal birds of prey.

FAMILY: *Accipitridae.*

GENUS: *Haliaeetus,* from Greek, haliaeetos, a bird, a sea eagle.

SPECIES: *Leucocephalus,* from Greek, leukos, white, and kephale, head.

TWO SUBSPECIES: *Haliaeetus leucocephalus leucocephalus,* found largely in Canada and Alaska, and *Haliaeetus leucocephalus alascanus,* primarily found south of the Canada-United States border.

SIZE: 34-43 inches long; body weight: male 8-9 lbs., female 10-14 lbs.; sex, age and geographic location influence the size and weight.

WINGSPREAD: 6-7$^{1}/_{2}$ feet.

RANGE: Alaska, Canada, around Great Lakes, south to Florida, Baja California.

COLORING: Adult (both sexes alike): snow-white head and tail; body brownish black; the large bill, eyes and feet bright yellow; immature: tail, head and body dark brown, less black than adult, some white on underside of wings; some plumage irregularly but extensively blotched with cream or white; bill is brownish, eyes pale yellow-gray; feet are lemon yellow and lower legs are naked of feathers on bottom half; tail and head become white when bird is 4 or 5 years old.

FLIGHT SPEED: Glide and flap in migration 36-44 miles per hour; 30 mph carrying fish.

LIFESPAN: In captivity, as long as fifty years; in the wild, a shorter life.

HABITAT: Seldom seen far from water (seacoasts, large rivers, lakes); also concentrated in national wildlife refuges and large reservoirs.

VOICE: Both sexes utter squealing, cackle, almost gull-like.

FEEDING HABITS: Mostly fish, waterfowl, muskrats, squirrels, rabbits.

NEST: As large as 7-8 feet across, 12 feet deep; built on rocky promontories, on ground, or in trees 10-150 feet off ground; sticks are foundation, lined with mosses, pine needles, grasses, feathers and other soft materials.

EGGS: 1-3, usually 2, dull white.

INCUBATION: 31-46 days; first flight of young 72-75 days after hatching.

MIGRATIONS: Motivated by changes in food supply — northern populations migrate furthest, southern eagles mainly stay in the same area.

FALL AND WINTER: Leave their roosts after dawn to go to favorite feeding perch, start feeding by swooping over the water and catching fish, then fly to other perching areas. Gather in groups where food is plentiful, highly social, roost with 2 to 500 eagles in same grove of trees, vocalize and fight over food. Inactive in cold weather; on clear days soar about if wind is right, then return to roost before dark.

SPRING AND SUMMER: Majority of time roosting, perching and loafing, and short periods of flight and brief hunting every one or two days.

Fused hand and fingers

Thumb

wrist

Radius and Ulna

Elbow

Humerus

Scapula

Breast bone

Tibia and Fibula

Heel

10 primaries (Primary Feathers) - can be spread out like the fingers on a hand to reduce drag.

Lesser coverts

Coverts - make the wing thicker in front, so that air will flow faster over the top of the wings.

16 to 18 Secondaries (Secondary Feathers) - can be moved down to increase drag or up to reduce it.

Axillaries

Pelvis

End of tail-bone

© Tot Ortega 1988

note: Entire skeleton of a Bald Eagle weighs only a little more than half a pound. The weight of the Eagle body is about 9 pounds.. (average weight)

note: Anatomy of the Eagle

upper tail coverts

12 tail feathers

Wﬁith silver braids
spanning an eagle's age,
the wise man recounts when the
white-headed bird watched the first
humans arrive in this ancient land:
    how the Eskimo crossed a frozen sea,
and the Hopi emerged from the earth.

        He tells how the Sky Woman
fell through the racial memory
of the Ho-de-no-sau-nee.

And when the sea rose over the land
and waves pounded against cliffs,
it was the eagle, he explains,
 who rescued a woman
    who gave birth to twins
and the origin of the Lakota people.

The spirit of the eagle spoke
in a boy's vision —
and the sacred wonder of it all
        can rekindle
    the spirits of all our nations.

White Deer of Autumn

For centuries,
the image of the
white-headed eagle
evoked the visions
and compelled the
aspirations of the Native American.
The eagle was the foremost reminder of the
Indian's guardianship responsibility to the land.
Such an honorable attribute as well as the
attained greatness of the Native American
have often been unknown, misunderstood,
or burlesqued in this land now dominated
by other races and ideologies.
Few people know that the eagle
symbol of the United States of America,
for example, was originally the symbol of the
League of the Ho-de-no-sau-nee, or Iroquois.
The transplant American borrowed the League's
symbol of the eagle, including the bound arrows
which equal
the number
of nations
and symbolize
their union.
He also borrowed ideas of democracy from the
People of the Longhouse.

White Deer of Autumn

Once, as mist clouds thickened
and rose from the mountain breasts at day's birth,
a boy gazed up at him, circling and spiraling
through the magic of time
and the power of silence.
Reeling and whirling on currents of wind,
the boy watched him, and his emotions waxed full
as if the moon were tugging on them.
Wise ones understood.
They told the boy that seeking visions this way
was a means he too could understand.
Thus, the boy was there, gazing at the eagle watching,
penetrating his center in the pale, early light
and all the while connecting circles in the cold sky.

He didn't know how long the eagle had spun
the moist, white fog into wisps of misty clouds,
but he did see him ultimately descend from them
and perch atop a jagged jewel of ice,
set in the sapphire waters of life.
And, still, eagle eyes fixed his eyes . . .
bright and strong like the sun,
they would not let the boy go.

This is how Misty Dawn became a man
and received his name,
and learned the stories that give origin to identity.

White Deer of Autumn

They don't look at us;
        they see into us!
    An eagle's stare
    from an icy sky
    or bare bough
        pierces like a laser.

The mystery-dark circles
    centered in the yellow iris
        of his eyes
        focus keenly.

Visionary power concentrated,
    they have, indeed, penetrated
    the center of man's being.

White Deer of Autumn

Among the Plains Indians, considered by many historians to be the greatest warriors on horseback in the world, the eagle also played a dominant role. Being students of nature as all Indians were, the native people of the North American Plains were driven to acts of bravery, in part, by the influence of the eagle. For in order to wear an eagle feather, a warrior had to have earned it in battle by killing an enemy. But the influence of nature's greatest bird did not stop with deliberate acts of courage in battle. Such aspirations alone could be detrimental to a nation's welfare. The Plains warrior, driven to adorn himself with the glory of eagle feathers but wise enough not to attempt self-extermination, developed a way of fighting so sophisticated and challenging that modern civilized nations may never achieve anything comparable. This was the fighting system of "counting coups."

As the primal mind of the Native American developed, he soon realized the horrors of bloody conflict. The wails of women and children over lost husbands, sons and fathers were not harmonious sounds among the waves of green grass where magpies sang and buffalo freely roamed. Bloody territorial conflicts were simply not supported by the wiser four legged and winged beings of the earth and sky. So, when fighting was the last resort after all words had failed, the warriors would face each other in territorial battles with as much ferocity as in the past and accompanied by the same fierce desire to win the eagle feathers. There was, however, a significant difference.

The idea of counting coups had developed into the practice of not killing in battle. It was rather the delivery of a swift blow or strike with a coup stick to an opponent's vital area that rendered the victim humiliated. That humiliation, though painfully inflicted, would force him off the battlefield a loser, but alive! Occasionally a warrior would die of such a wound in territorial conflict, but not often. And there was no intent to kill in battle any longer; that is, until the transplant Americans arrived with guns.

It is fascinating what nature and her greatest winged creature had inspired in our native people. The true glory of winning the prized eagle feather among the Plains warriors did not render women without husbands, children without fathers, mothers without sons. Indeed, much has been misunderstood about the men who wore eagle feathers and the cultures the American eagle influenced.

White Deer of Autumn

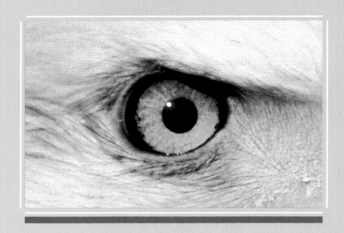

Probably even in legend
his marvelous power of vision
has not been exaggerated.
Those fierce and haughty eyes,
gleaming so sternly
under their overhanging brows,
are in truth as keen as they look
and are able to pick out small objects
at incredible distances.

Such magnificent visual acuity
is characteristic of birds of prey,
which possess the best vision
in the world of vertebrates.
The soaring eagle can see
the form of a cottontail crouching so far away
that the human eye would see nothing but grass,
and can detect the movement of a fish
close to the surface.

An eagle's vision is roughly that of a man
looking through six-power binoculars.
This is not so much because the eagle's eyes magnify,
but because they give a clearer picture.

George Laycock

The most sacred object among North American Indians is the Pipe, and it is an object only when the bowl and stem are separated. Fit together, it is a living being. There were and still are Pipes used for unique purposes. And though these may vary from war to peace, one essential aspect of all Pipes is primary: the Pipe is used to address the Great Holy Mystery. It is the word made physical. So holy and regarded was the Pipe that an individual could carry a Calumet, the most sacred of all tribal Pipes, across this land with complete impunity. Even in the heat of battle, men would lay down their weapons before the Pipe. It is understandable why certain items fastened to Pipe stems are of great religious significance. Among those special ornaments and elements of power are eagle feathers.

Tied to the Pipe, the eagle feathers represent the winged nations of the world. When words are spoken with the Pipe, they transcend into the smoke, and are carried swiftly to their intended source by the power evoked by the eagle feathers. Ultimately, the words become one with all things.

I remember one Pipe whose keeper placed an eagle feather where the bowl and the stem were fixed together. He explained that this was a medicine Pipe used for healing not only physical wounds but wounds of the heart and mind as well. Another Pipe keeper tied an eagle's white tail feather right near the mouthpiece of the stem. He said that this was the feather of sincerity and purity of words. Indeed! For no Indian would ever lie while holding a Pipe, and all agreements were sealed by this formal smoking and binding of a man's word, committed in the presence of the eagle's feather.

White Deer of Autumn

Alone together!
Neither colonial nor social, bald eagles,
when they gather to watch the winter waterways,
solemnly preside over earth and sky
in unison with an icy splendor and authority
that invite no challenge.
From their powerful presence,
which brooks no mortal thoughts nor sacrilege,
emanates an elemental majesty and mysticism
revered by man primeval since he first set foot
on these American shores.
The hoary mane and snowy tail, tokens of wisdom,
cast their own enlightening spell
as they tell of age and full maturity
at three or four or even five.

Stanwyn G. Shetler

Down through time many great minds,
including Leonardo da Vinci, have speculated on the
marvel of the feather and the miracle of flight,
whose evolution still remains largely a mystery.
In a feather at rest, one sees not the shape
that will be used in flying, but a design
that will automatically achieve shapes
in response to different pressures from the air.

John H. Storer

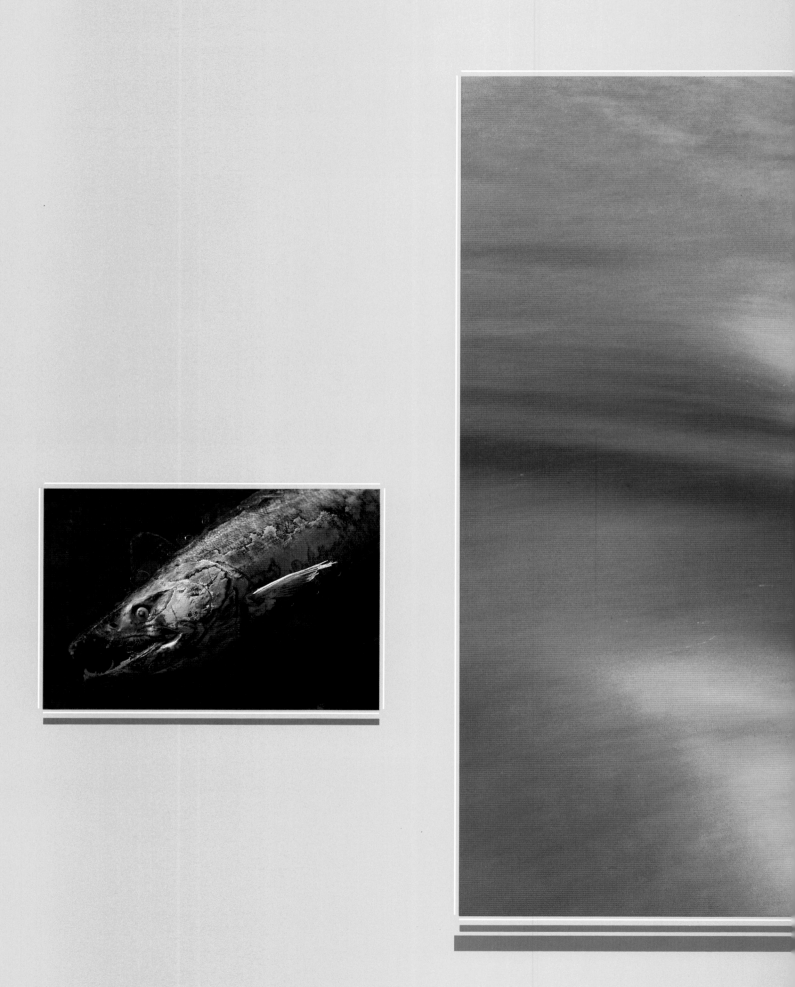

Having traveled widely in its search for food,
and located it, perhaps at an amazing distance,
the eagle must also possess equipment
for capturing and killing its prey.
The instant the eagle's talons touch its prey,
powerful tendons flex and draw the toes tight,
driving the needle-pointed talons inward toward each other,
where they remain locked.
Tiny projecting spikes on the bottoms of the toes
also aid in gripping slippery fish.

George Laycock

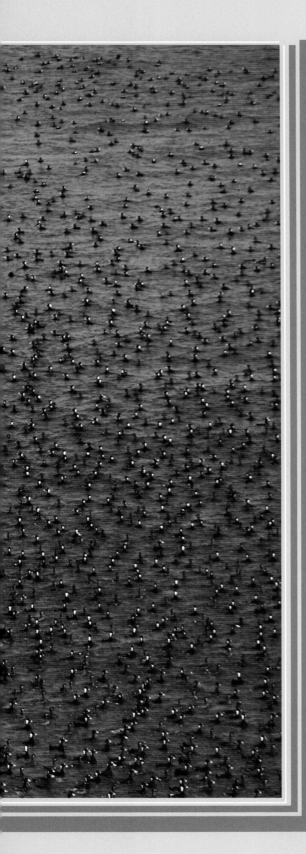

The shallow waters of the river flats were packed and crammed with life. From farther south, regiment after regiment of wild ducks had come in: big, burly-bodied mallards, compact, keen-winged teal, slim, graceful pintails, already beginning by easy stages their long journey to the far northern breeding grounds. The sunlight, striking downward through the morning mists, glittered on a thousand iridescent green heads, illumined the snowy breasts and necks of the pintail squadrons, lit the white cheek crescents of the blue-winged teal. More numerous even than the ducks, a multitude of coots moved here and there along the reedy margins, their blue-black heads bobbing awkwardly as they swam, their white bills gleaming like polished nickel.

A half mile upstream the river swung to the west in a sharp curve where a long narrow peninsula, densely wooded with tall pines, thrust outward halfway across the flats. Suddenly, from behind this promontory, a dark shape sailed into view — a great white-headed eagle, planing on motionless pinions some sixty feet above the surface of the water.

For half a minute nothing happened. Then swiftly the panorama was transformed. The life that crowded the flooded flats, the feathered fleets that had been floating idly there, awoke to instant activity. Near the pine promontory the surface of the lagoon heaved upward, while at the same moment a surging, rushing sound filled the air. Directly in front of the eagle a flock of mallards had risen with a drumming thunder of pinions; and that thunder was a signal to all the vari-colored multitude thronging that watery world.

Squadron after squadron,
regiment after regiment,
the wild duck armies
lifted from the surface.
The air shook with the
swelling roar of their wings,
with the palpitant clamor
of companies of coots
scurrying
madly across the water.

Swiftly the teeming flats were emptying themselves of life.
In a tumult of whirring wings and a turmoil of pattering, splashing feet,
the legions of the waterfowl were fleeing before their master and sovereign . . . .
And that drumming thunder of wings that rolled before him down the flats
as the wild duck regiments took flight at his approach
was his vassals' tribute to his power.

Herbert Sass

There is the sound when the wind calls
and the splash of the fish as they jump
to accompany the roar of the waterfall
leading from the lake that I love
To be where no man has stood before
to camp in a virgin stand
to gaze at the heavens where eagles soar
at one with this unspoiled land
To see grassy meadows where honkers nest
to hear the cry of the loon
or watching bear with their salmon catch
in a river south of Angoon

Richard Cohn

For all lovers of the outdoors, to whom Nature's wildness is perhaps her most alluring charm, the sight of an eagle in the sky is ample reward for many days of seeking; and when it happens to them that day after day and week after week the king of birds has a place in the panorama of wildlife witnessed on trips afield, they know that they are living through days that will not be forgotten.

There was one day when I saw eagle matched against eagle, not in battle, but in a contest only less stirring than actual battle would have been. Far away across the marshlands I saw an eagle hurrying toward the sea. He was flying at high speed, his dark wings powerfully beating the air; and, in a few moments, I saw behind him another eagle also rushing at utmost speed toward the ocean. I looked seaward in the direction in which the two great white-headed birds were flying, but I could distinguish nothing there; yet I judged from the manner and the velocity of their flight that their keen eyes saw what I did not or could not see.

The leading eagle, which was some hundreds of yards ahead of the other, crossed the narrow strip of beach between the marshes and the ocean, heading straight out over the Atlantic; then, suddenly, I saw in front of him, well out over the water, an osprey circling and spiraling upward. At that distance I could not discern the fish in the osprey's claws, but I knew that it was there — that this was the prize which had brought the two monarchs hurrying across the marshlands from their lookout stations perhaps a mile or several miles away.

I knew what would happen, for I had seen it often before; but this time the sequel was a surprise. The osprey, a large and strong-winged hawk, often fights hard to keep his fish, circling upward, dodging and twisting, refusing to surrender until his last chance of escape has gone. This osprey, however, gave up quickly. At the first swoop of the eagle the sea hawk dropped his fish, and the larger bird, shooting downward with half-closed wings, seized it in his talons before it struck the surface of the water.

He did not keep it long. The other eagle, arriving at this moment upon the scene, drove at him with furious speed, and for a few minutes I saw a thrilling contest in the air above the ocean — the two great birds swooping and swerving, dodging and twisting this way and that, the one trying to escape, the other and apparently more powerful bird cutting him off at every turn. If these eagles were mates, perhaps the male had taken the fish from the osprey only to give it to his consort; in that case, this mad chase above the ocean was only a game — a phase, perhaps, of the eagles' autumnal love-making. But to my eyes it had all the appearance of deadly earnestness, and, in any case, it was, while it lasted, perhaps the finest display of this sort that I have witnessed. It was too furious to last long. Presently the first eagle released the fish, and the other, with a magnificent downward gliding swoop, caught it in her talons and bore it off through the air.

That was a fine, wild, stirring sight, and one not often seen. Yet when I think of all the pictures of eagles printed upon my memory during those blue and white and golden autumn days, there is a picture of another kind that comes to the fore.

I was looking across a belt of marshland toward the strip of beach and the ocean beyond when I saw an eagle hovering above the waves perhaps a hundred yards beyond the outermost billows of the surf. Almost at once this eagle was joined by another; and for a long while, perhaps a quarter of an hour, the two big birds, both of them adults with white heads and tails, were engaged with something, invisible to me, on or near the surface of the water, which completely absorbed their attention.

They were fishing, I concluded, after I had watched them for some time. Probably a school of small fish, menhaden perhaps, was moving near the surface, or possibly something was floating there that might serve the eagles as food. They circled back and forth low above the water, or hung just over it with slowly beating wings, now and again swooping down to it, not with the speed of the osprey but with a statelier gliding motion, never plunging beneath the surface, as the osprey often does, but evidently striking at their prey with their claws. Whatever it was that they sought, it was not easily secured; and I was glad of this, for, although there was nothing especially dramatic in the spectacle, it was to me a scene of extraordinary interest and beauty, and I would not willingly have lost a minute of it.

It was afternoon, and there was something, some power or quality, in the slanting rays of the sun that deepened and intensified all the rich colors of land and sea. The marsh over which I gazed was a glorious bronze-gold and the sea beyond was a deep, intense blue; yet at the same time, by that magic of the late light, all bright colors seemed to be made brighter, so that the white parallel lines of the surf were a most brilliant white against the blue of the water and the white heads and tails of the eagles shone with the glittering whiteness of snow.

As they hovered just above the surface, their snowy tails spread wide, their white heads and necks bent downward, the light seemed to shine through them, and their broad wings appeared no longer dark brown or black but a lighter, almost translucent brown tinged with gold. Viewed thus, they lacked the stateliness of the eagle on high, the majesty of the eagle in swift pursuit across the heavens. Yet there was a beauty in them that was royal and splendid; and those two eagles, lit by the sun and poised above the blue water, seemed to me then, and seem to me still, one of the finest pictures of wildlife that I have ever seen.

Herbert Sass

She traced the eagle wing impression
on the snowy earth with her pale, wrinkled fingers.
She imagined it was like touching his ghost.
The clarity of memory that accompanies age fascinated her.
Playing in tracks as a girl and now full circle
she finds herself once again, remembering . . . .

It was not long after she began her journey in the circle of life
that she saw the eagle. A wave of wind caught him
and carried him higher than he'd ever been.
He screamed in exhilaration and she sighed in awe.

Every autumn he left her a feather
until she had a fan with the power of his wing.
It impacted everything: her marriage, the birth of her children . . .
and death: first, her wise uncle, then her mom, her dad,
a brother, a sister, one child, her mother-in-law,
and now her husband.
And all that's left is the impression of things going in circles,
like when she saw the young eagle soar,
and they became aware of themselves.

There was no feather this fall,
only the impression of things going full circle.

White Deer of Autumn

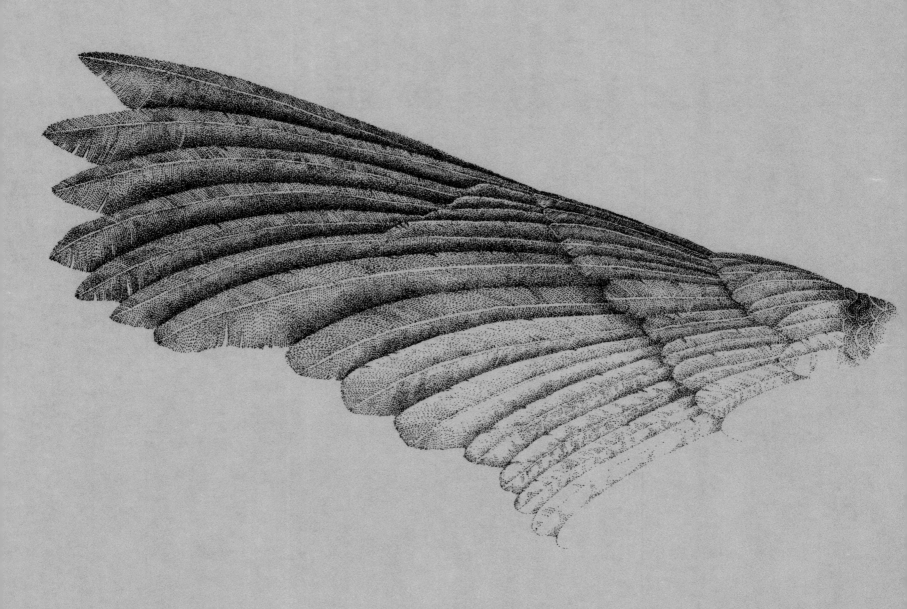

"Cac-cac-cac . . ."
"Kek-kek-kek . . ."
floating down to us
as we watched.

Like the crowing
of a chanticleer,
the eagle's scream
is perhaps a signal,
as well as a challenge
and note of defiance.

Francis Hobart Herrick

Bald eagles,
    seemingly oblivious to frigid weather,
may pass the winter wherever they breed, north or south,
    as long as there is open water for hunting.
But many migrate along time-honored routes,
    as along the northeast-southwest ridges
    converging at Pennsylvania's famed Hawk Mountain,
        to time-honored winter havens.

    Eagles of the northern race,
        breeding in Alaska, Canada and the northern tier of states,
fly south in the fall to California, the Mississippi Valley
        and the Chesapeake Bay region,
            returning north again in spring.
In a reverse pattern, the southern eagles, as immatures,
fly or (shall we say) drift north from their breeding grounds,
        notably in Florida, as far as Prince Edward Island
    (according to banding studies), and then return in the fall.
These, presumably, are the southward-bound bald eagles
that sail by the craggy promontories on Hawk Mountain
    in late August and early September —
        fleeting glimpses of lordly beauty in review.

Stanwyn G. Shetler

Sometimes bald eagles and bears —
black and brown — share the fishing, as
in the salmon-spawning streams and rivers
of Alaska and the Pacific Northwest. Here
both prey upon the rich supply of salmon
that are running, the eagles tending to
go for the spent and dying females that
have already spawned. Perhaps as many
as 15,000 bald eagles of the northern race
are resident in this region during the
breeding season in a population long
sustained by the abundance of fish. Only
here is the bald eagle so common as to be
taken for granted. Along the Chilkat River,
where a bald eagle refuge has been created,
several thousand eagles can be seen at one
time in season.

The magnificent birds may be
present at times in unreal numbers,
especially along the salmon-filled
waterways. Several to a dozen or more
may perch on the icy or gravelly shores
or festoon the snags and large coniferous
trees like ornaments on a Christmas tree.
In winter, their white pates and tails blend
in to the snowy landscape and snow-
covered bare branches. And in summer,
their snow-capped heads may echo in
miniature in the foreground the snow-
capped peaks of massive lofty mountains
in the background. Despite the huge
disparity in scale, the eagles do not yield
one little bit to the massifs in their
dominion or grandeur in this incalculable
land. In the misty early morning light or
the last rays of sunset, eagle-ladened trees
present surreal, mystic images against a
shining ice-clad mountain
or glowing sky.

Stanwyn G. Shetler

With singular majesty and power,
the bald eagle, North America's largest native eagle,
symbolizes both a nation and a continent.
Because it is widely recognized as America's flying emblem,
this raptor, more than any other single species around the world,
carries the flag for the wildlife of an entire continent.

With its mighty six-foot wing span and every primary splayed out,
as it reconnoiters, like a flying fortress,
along some rugged coastal frontier,
the eagle is a study in
the anatomy of flight.

Stanwyn G. Shetler

Beautiful bird
fly beyond our dreams
soar where the stars
intrigue our gaze
and challenge
the mystery of the unknown
Let your wings
unbound the limits
of our thoughts
and warm the chill
beyond our earth
with the beauty
of your soul

Richard Cohn

Beautiful bird
fly beyond our dreams
soar where the stars
intrigue our gaze
and challenge
the mystery of the unknown
Let your wings
unbound the limits
of our thoughts
and warm the chill
beyond our earth
with the beauty
of your soul

Richard Cohn

And when the time came to choose a symbol for the new American nation, to represent its spirit, its essence, its vision, the founders of our country chose the American Bald Eagle. Bold. Courageous. Vigilant. Free. Native Americans had long regarded the eagle as a messenger between heaven and earth, as a carrier of information from the Great Spirit to those who walked upon this world. So it was a fitting symbol for the country that already upon its Seal had inscribed the words: *Novus Ordo Seclorum.* What better creature to share that Great Seal than the messenger between heaven and earth? What better symbol than the eagle to represent the bridging of eternity's promise and mortal man's daily struggle?

If a New Order of the Ages was truly to be born upon North American soil, as the founders of our nation prayed, then it would be because the people of this new nation embodied qualities well symbolized by the eagle. It would be in that supreme balance between vigilance and innocence, between trust and certainty, between the sun and the mountain crags below, in that communion, in that synthesis, that the New Order would emerge. It would be upon eagle's wings that a new vision would enter — and forever alter — human affairs.

Five generations. The American Eagle has watched.

Peoples of all tribes, cultures and races have left the far continents of the world to come to these cooperative states. To stay. To become Americans, working, playing, praying, raising their children together. Sharing their dreams, their hopes, their fears, their passions and desires, becoming one people, one tribe, one nation, under God.

America is an example to the world, not for superficial government policy, but for the blending of races and peoples that occurs daily on her street corners, in her marketplaces, in her schools, churches and factories. The reunion of the tribes is significant, for in the willingness of the once-scattered peoples of the earth to join together and interact as a single nation, it is as though the missing pieces of some awesome unit were once again coming together, as though the scattered systems and cells of some vast and unspeakable magnificence were being slowly assembled.

To the degree that America's people have overcome their differences and embraced cooperation, America has prospered. To the degree that they have failed, the New Order remains still in process — conceived and growing to be sure, but not yet truly arrived.

For what is struggling toward birth in these United States was not conceived in Boston or in Philadelphia — nor on earth at all — but in the air of an Eternal Spirit. With each new generation, it comes forth yet further, then further, then further still, until its emergence is no longer measured in generations, nor even in years, but in months, weeks — and yes, day by day.

Perhaps even now
  it is but a movement,
a moment,
  a last wingbeat away. ▧

Ken Carey

In 1776, the rebellious thirteen colonies that lay along the eastern seaboard of a great, unexplored territory in North America found themselves near to achieving a long-desired goal: independence.

They looked for a symbol, one which would evoke a definite expression of liberty, the ideal for which they had fought and the principle upon which their new government would be founded.

The eagle had long been a prominent symbol among the native tribes of North America — it may have been an unconscious impetus that suggested this newly dominant tribe focus its attention on the same bird. Or it may have been the reputation that the eagle had built for himself in legend.

It may have been simply that, although eagles are inhabitants of foreign lands, only two species are known in the United States — the American bald eagle and the golden eagle — and of these two, the bald eagle is both more abundant (found at one time in every state in the Union) and unknown outside of North America. But whether our forefathers were swayed by nationalistic or indigenous or romantic notions, it is certainly true that the American bald eagle was chosen as our national symbol almost as early as there was a nation in existence.

A symbol is something that exists as itself on a literal level and at the same time suggests something larger, something perhaps more important. Symbols are expressions of desire, purpose, ideals. As such, the eagle has come to mean many things to many people throughout recorded history. More than any other quality, however, mankind seems to respond to the eagle's spirit, wild and free, and this has generated for the eagle a symbolic status shared by few other animals.

The eagle has appeared in numerous other contexts that carry political or nationalistic significance, including many forms of American currency, both old and new, not the least of which are the gold coins which carried the bird as part of their name: eagle, half eagle, quarter eagle, and double eagle.

And today, the eagle's symbolic nature has expanded again, to include one more element which speaks to us clearly: the eagle is a lingering reminder of the pristine and vast wilderness that was once North America. It is a symbol of a not-so-distant past when birds and animals — not excluding man — lived as an integral part of their environment. An endangered species still, despite legislation to stop the trend, the American bald eagle, in a sense, represents each American more thoroughly than ever. Each individual bird is powerful, independent, courageous . . . but the species as a whole is poised on the edge of annihilation.

Perhaps if the bald eagle can be saved,
     so too can the soul of mankind
          which, for centuries, this bird has symbolized.

Gay Monteverde

Only two of the many familiar American symbols have been deliberately created by law — the flag and the Great Seal. The design of the Great Seal was the result of an astonishing amount of work by some of the most famous of early American patriots — including two future presidents. On July 4, 1776, only a few hours after the signing of the Declaration of Independence, the Continental Congress formed a committee comprised of Benjamin Franklin, John Adams and Thomas Jefferson to create the seal of the new United States of America. The creative process was a ponderous one, however. Over a period of six years, the design went through three major and numerous minor revisions, including the well-known story of Franklin's suggestion that the national bird be a turkey.

In the end, the committee, whether suspicious of Franklin's reputation for wry humor or vainly incapable of seeing themselves in a bird as unheroic and ungraceful as a turkey, chose the American bald eagle as the nation's symbol.

The Great Seal was to include the eagle "displayed" to amplify the image of strength, independence, and victory. On its breast appeared the armorial shield with thirteen red and white stripes and a blue horizontal panel above them, symbolizing the interdependence of the thirteen states and the Congress above them. The right talon of the eagle grasped the olive branch, symbolizing the power to make peace; the left talon held thirteen arrows, one for each of the original colonies, symbolizing the power to make war. In its bill, the eagle held a scroll with the motto *"E Pluribus Unum,"* which means "Out of many, one." Over its head was a "constellation of thirteen stars surrounded with bright rays and, at a little distance, clouds."

On June 20, 1782, with the end of the war for independence imminent and the need for a sovereign seal with which to sign a treaty becoming urgent, the Congress finally adopted the bald eagle as the symbol of the United States. This emblem, which has changed very little in 200 years, still appears on the Great Seal of the United States, on the President's flag, and on the President's seal in the bronze plate on the floor of the vestibule of the White House.

One of nature's unique gifts to North America, the bald eagle once thrived throughout most of the continent. Today, as a breeding bird, it survives mainly along the southern coast of Alaska to British Columbia and along the west coast of Florida, but also in lesser strongholds, most notably the Chesapeake Bay and Great Lakes regions.

When in 1782 the Continental Congress selected the bald eagle as the national emblem of the new American republic, the esteemed representatives could not have foreseen, or even imagined, the mortal perils that would one day befall the eagle and decimate its ranks almost to the vanishing point before rescue efforts would begin to pull the species back from the brink of oblivion. Irresponsible as it now seems, looking back on the many decades of complacency and open season and the manic pesticide explosion of the 1950s and 1960s when DDT and its chemical relatives threatened to extinguish not only the raptors but many other birds (indeed, in the words of Rachel Carson, to silence spring forever), the bald eagle's future welfare was taken for granted for more than 150 years and no national protection was afforded.

Such was the ecological ignorance and conservation indifference of those years that the bald eagle and birds of prey in general were stigmatized as varmints of nature because they killed beneficial songbirds, fish and game, and sometimes domestic poultry and livestock.

They were righteously pursued and destroyed, often with an official price on their heads. For the bald eagle, this shameful state lasted until 1940 when the federal Bald Eagle Protection Act was passed, although the Act did not at the time cover Alaska, where bounties were paid until 1953. In Alaska alone, bounty hunters, who viewed the piscivorous bald eagle as a threat to their fishing livelihoods, cashed in more than 100,000 eagles in one period of less than 20 years before 1940.

Owing to the heavy use of DDT and related pesticides, persistent chlorinated hydrocarbons accumulated in the waters and in the fish, ultimately concentrating in the eagles at the top of the food chain, poisoning them and reducing or destroying their ability to reproduce. The eggs became infertile or thin-shelled and highly susceptible to crushing during incubation. In a few short years whole populations became sterile, their nesting success dropping nearly to zero. Immature birds all but disappeared from some migrating corridors and wintering concentrations, especially in the east. Only the Alaskan population remained relatively healthy. Around the shores of the Chesapeake Bay, where in better days hundreds of pairs nested (perhaps as many as a thousand when America belonged to the Indians), the nesting population crashed to a low ebb of about three dozen pairs.

Fortunately, the disaster was discovered before it was too late, use of DDT was banned, and heroic eleventh-hour steps were taken to rescue the bald eagle and other imperiled species from certain doom.

Rescue, restoration and conservation efforts got underway in earnest in the 1970s through the concerted efforts of many conservation organizations and state and federal agencies. The National Wildlife Federation in particular, with the aid of private corporations, mounted a major campaign to raise public awareness, increase the information base, and spur conservation action. Money was raised to buy refuges. With spectacular success, the national emblem became also the emblem of an entire environmental revolution.

Today, although still endangered over much of its range, the bald eagle, as a species, is on the road to recovery. Almost everywhere the signs are good. The species enjoys general protection, public respect, and safe haven in a number of strategic, newly established refuges on the continent.

Breeding populations are stabilized or on the rise. The Chesapeake Bay breeding population, for example, is back up in the neighborhood of a hundred nests. And once again this majestic bird is not an uncommon sight along the Potomac River in the vicinity of Washington, D.C., where one may on occasion see it cruising up or down the river or soaring in lazy circles overhead. Indeed, a pair only recently renewed the bald eagle's lease on the territory by nesting several years in a row on an island in the Potomac just above Great Falls after years of nesting no farther up the river than Mason Neck near Mount Vernon.

It is doubtful that the species will ever recover to the point of being completely out of danger. Apart from the ever-present hazard of pollution and the poisoning of its food supply, habitat disturbance or destruction through human encroachment and lawless killing are relentless threats to the eagle. The southern race is especially sensitive to human disturbance, spooking easily during the nesting season unless given a very wide berth. Ever-accelerating development is wiping out more and more of the requisite big trees and original, secluded sites for nesting. Perpetual vigilance is the only key to the eagles' future welfare.

Stanwyn G. Shetler
National Museum of Natural History
Smithsonian Institution

Eagle Restoration and Rehabilitation Programs

If you are interested in restoration or rehabilitation of bald eagles, you might consider contacting the following organizations. Your help and support will be greatly appreciated.

National Fish and
Wildlife Foundation
Room 2626
18th & C Streets N.W.
Washington, DC 20240
(202) 343-1040

The Nature Conservancy
1815 Lynn Street
Arlington, VA 22209
(703) 841-5300

Raptor Rehabilitation and
Propagation Project, Inc.
Tyson Research Center
Box 193
Eureka, MO 63025
(314) 938-6193

Raptor Research and
Rehabilitation Program
College of Veterinary Medicine
University of Minnesota
St. Paul, MN 55108
(612) 624-4745

Save Our American Raptors
(SOAR) Inc.
802 Hemlock Drive
Apopka, FL 32712
(407) 889-3962

Save The Eagle Project
P.O. Box 8118
Mt. Juliet, TN 37122
(615) 885-7000

George Miksch Sutton
Avian Research Center, Inc.
P.O. Box 2007
Bartlesville, OK 74005-2007
(918) 336-7778

University of Florida
Department of Wildlife
Range Services
Gainesville, FL 32611-0301
(904) 392-4851

Woodland Park
Zoological Gardens
5500 Phinney Ave. N.
Seattle, WA 98103
(206) 684-4800

World Wildlife Fund
1255 Twenty-Third Street
Washington, DC 20037
(202) 293-4800

For additional information on bald eagles, contact The American Bald Eagle Foundation, Box 49, Haines, AK 99827, (907) 766-2549; Raptor Education Foundation, 21901 E. Hampden Ave., Aurora, CO 80013, (303) 680-8500; or your state Department of Conservation or Department of Fish and Wildlife Management.

There was a time when bald eagles were a common sight across the American land. No one had to go to extraordinary lengths to see our national symbol in the wild. Today, though still widespread on the continent, the bald eagle is so localized as to be generally rare, and spotting one is a special treat.

Now, wherever they occur, eagles are the resident celebrities of the habitat and top the birdwatcher's pecking order of "good" birds to see when visiting such localities. Below you will find listed some of the main areas for viewing the American bald eagle in its natural habitat.

Location	State	Optimum Viewing
Chilkat River Bald Eagle Preserve	Alaska	All year
Bear Valley National Wildlife Refuge	California	Winter
San Luis Valley, Rio Grande	Colorado	Winter
Everglades National Park	Florida	All year
Prairie State Eagle Refuge	Illinois	All year
Chesapeake Bay	Maryland	All year
Swan Lake National Wildlife Refuge	Missouri	Winter
Glacier National Park	Montana	Winter
Klamath Lake National Wildlife Refuge	Oregon	Winter
Karl Mundt National Wildlife Refuge	South Dakota	Winter
Reelfoot National Wildlife Refuge	Tennessee	Winter
San Juan Islands	Washington	All year
Olympic National Park	Washington	All year
Skagit River Bald Eagle Natural Area	Washington	Winter
Eagle Valley Sanctuary	Wisconsin	Winter
Vancouver Island	Canada	All year

When we began taking wildlife photographs twelve years ago neither of us knew how our photography or our business relationship would evolve. What we've found is that we both have our own vision. Pat is a contemplative photographer who lives to check the composition, the exposure setting and other photographic nuances many times before taking a photo. I am a motor drive addict who brackets excessively and tends to shoot his way into photographs.

While taking photos for this book, we had eagles swoop down within several feet of our heads, got "sea sick" sitting in a blind in the top of a wind-swaying fir tree, became stranded in a remote wilderness area when a camp stove overturned (burning most of our camping gear and food), and pitched our tent next to an active bear trail.

For us, hard work has always been the most important ingredient in fine wildlife photography. "Being there" was far more important than equipment brands or F-stops. Being there means getting out of the warm sleeping bag and in position before sunrise, staying the extra day, hiking the extra mile, sitting out the storm. Being there is the actual time spent in an animal's territory. Professional technique, filters, remote control units, extra-long lenses are all important tools, but nothing can be substituted for time spent with the animal through all the seasons in all kinds of weather. Then the magic happens.

We use Nikon equipment with lenses ranging from 20mm to 600mm. For the eagles, we frequently added a 1.4 teleconverter to the 600, making this lens an 840mm. We average 800 rolls of film (or slightly less than 30,000 images) per year using Kodachrome 64, Fujichrome 50 and Fujichrome 100.

To enable us to "be there" during nesting we used a custom-built blind with a metal grid platform three feet square and a bar supporting a (very) small seat. A chain around the trunk holds the blind in place. A collapsible framework of metal rods was added to hold taut the camouflage material. This blind is lightweight, portable and reusable.

To install the blind high in a tree Pat pulled it up by rope while I pushed and guided it through the limbs from underneath. Somewhat hesitantly I stepped out on the small grid platform to piece together the rods for the camouflage material with 80 feet of open space below me. Completed, the blind seemed like a secure, snug little room, making it easy to forget that if one of us dropped a pen (or, worse, a lens) it couldn't easily be retrieved.

When we think of the weeks we spent alternating shifts every three to four hours in the blind, the memories are not of the obvious discomforts but of the special moments, the intimate glimpses into the natural world made possible only by our invisible perch high in the top of a conifer.

People often ask if we are afraid when we are out. We've had a few moments of racing heartbeats and shaking limbs. Those are the situations that make the great stories we're saving to tell our children. We find fear comes from being caught by surprise in a situation we aren't prepared to handle. Because knowledge and careful planning are our best defense, we discuss potential dangers before we begin a new wildlife assignment. We often carry with us a pepper-derivative animal repellent, an air horn, halizone tablets and a first-aid kit. Most importantly, as we walk into the wilderness we also carry with us our past experiences, which have shown us that most wildlife, even bears and snakes, do not desire a direct confrontation with humans and will do their part to avoid it if one remains sensitive to their subtle cues. Instead of fear, we find the presence of danger develops in us increased awareness and a sense of being and moving in harmony with our surroundings.

One of the many locations we visited while photographing this book was the Chilkat River in southeast Alaska. The best eagle photography here occurs between late October and late December, and the best conditions are when arctic air moves down over the region, freezing the freshwater streams and lakes. The eagles are forced to concentrate along a few miles of the Chilkat River where a natural upwelling of water prevents the river from completely freezing over.

This can be an uncomfortable time to be a photographer. Cooped up in the van, one can wait through weeks of dreary, rainy days for the "good" cold weather. Once it does get cold, my fingers threaten to lose the sensitivity needed to operate the camera. But when one has the opportunity to see several hundred eagles at a time, to watch the first light of day brush the top of Four Winds Mountain with the palest pink hue, intensify to a brilliant glow, then gradually subside to the harsh blue-white of daytime sky, one revels in the virile joy of being a part of a harsh, yet intensely beautiful, moment. Waiting at such times is only a part of the reverence one owes in return for being alive on a new day in a wild place.

Tom and Pat Leeson

Photographers' Acknowledgments

During the years we've photographed wildlife, we've come to appreciate eagles as one of God's most dynamic creations, and it is with thanksgiving and joy that we share this intimate glimpse into the life of this fascinating bird.

We are pleased to acknowledge the vision, dedication, hard work, patience and loving support of all with whom we worked.

Bob Goodman was the first to give us encouragement and a sense of where to begin.

Richard Cohn and Cindy Black, our publishers, took our dream and made it their dream, shaping it, guiding it, living it with us. Their sensitivity and insight frequently drew us together, keeping our focus strong. Their experience in publishing the highly acclaimed books *Within a Rainbowed Sea* and *Molokai: An Island in Time* was a gift of immeasurable value from which we richly benefited.

Dorothy Wieden, our designer, performed marvelously under an incredibly tight deadline and under extremely frustrating circumstances, literally working day and night. We cherish her graciousness as well as her creative energy.

Char and Byron Liske of Dynagraphics, Inc. have been friends, advisers, and now, at last, the printers of our book. They give of themselves in everything they do, another gift we treasure.

The assistance of Mary Lee Battaglia, Michael Bennett, Marcia Ely and Pam Lazoff, which impacted the project on a variety of levels, was invaluable.

In our search for bald eagles to photograph, several people eased our way: Peggy and Bill MacPherson; Isla, Jim and Gordon Broadfoot; Hugh Oakes; and Dave Menske and Denny Zwiedelhofer of the U.S. Fish and Wildlife Service.

Of the many who have nurtured us over the years, we especially remember with warmth and appreciation: Gene and Ruth Wade; Mrs. Geraldine Hansen; Minnie Schulz from our "Montana" days; Robert (Bob) Dunne, who published our first wildlife packages and, more importantly, gave us hope; John Nuhn; Tom Powell; Declan Haun; Tom Ulrich; Becky and Gary Vestal; Pat and Tina O'Hara; Vicki Hurst; Don, Pauline, Elise and Curt Daniel; Joe Palena; the staff at Tymers; Ila Young; Blanche DeMerice; and Don Clendenon.

A special thanks to Tom Kitchin, a friend and fellow photographer, who has shared ideas, camp spots and more pots of stew than either of us care to remember.

We are both grateful to our families for instilling in us a love of and respect for nature. Luther Clendenon demonstrated the joy of wilderness adventure. LeRoy Leeson introduced us to the skills, discipline and wildlife lore of the hunter.

Tom's mom, Betty Leeson Pritel, has been an anchor for us — stabilizing, encouraging, uplifting, supportive. Her unflinching and unfailing confidence in us has sustained us through many long years. Her love has been one of God's greatest gifts to us.

We appreciate the response of the wide variety of authors who lend this book the benefit of their experience and philosophy. While sometimes differing from our own views, we hope this kaleidoscope of thoughts — historical, spiritual, scientific, personal — blend to enrich the reader's visual experience.

Publisher's Acknowledgments

The publisher would like to express deep appreciation to everyone who has helped create *The American Eagle*: Tom and Pat Leeson for their superb photography and willingness to assist in every aspect of bringing their dream to fruition; Cynthia Black, my wife, editor and co-publisher, for her months of research and her love and support throughout this entire project; Dottie Wieden for her inspiring design, positive attitude and dedication to making the book the best it could be; our contributing writers, Ken Carey, White Deer of Autumn, Dr. Stanwyn Shetler, Dr. Michael Robinson and Gay Monteverde, whose poetic prose complements the visual experience of the photographic images; David Hillman for his careful proofreading; David Forester for his skill with the Macintosh and help with preparing the book; Debra Mecartea for her invaluable assistance in typesetting and text layout; Duane Hatnenn, Mike Running Wolf, John Brave Hawk and Bill Ray for assisting us with the Native American section of the book; all of the eagle restoration and rehabilitation organizations for educating and informing us, especially Steve Sherrod of George Miksch Sutton Avian Research Center, Inc. and Doris Mager of Save Our American Raptors; Aperture PhotoBank for allowing us to use some of their photos; Hot Shots for its superb eagle video and film duplication; Broadway Productions for all its help; Portland Advertising Typography, Inc. for excellent Linotronic output; the entire staff of Dynagraphics, Inc. for their commitment to quality printing and their continued support of our endeavors; everyone at Wy'east Color for fabulous color separations; Bob Bengtson at Lincoln and Allen, our bookbinder; Pat Ortega and Spencer Lewis for their artistry; Michelle Glazer for her countless hours of research; Diane True, Shirley Kopta and the "Hockey Mothers," our bookpackers; Jesus Sanchez of Sanchez Rivet, our Collector's Edition craftsman; Barbara Krumbholz of First Interstate Bank for her belief in us; Michael Bennett for his marketing skills; and Mary Battaglia, our valued assistant, for her unwavering dedication.

Publisher's Note

In many areas, photographing bald eagles at nest sites may require a special permit from the U.S. Fish and Wildlife Service. Permits are also required to possess bald eagle feathers and parts.

Photography Credits

Tom Bean/Aperture PhotoBank, pages 24, 25.

Lon Lauber, pages 27, 30, 46, 58-59.

Steve McCutcheon/Aperture Photobank, page 81.

Nancy Simmerman/Aperture Photobank, pages 88, 89.

Frans Lanting, page 90.

Art Wolfe/Aperture PhotoBank, page 97.

Department of the Navy, United States Naval Academy Museum, Annapolis, Maryland. "River Queen Eagle," a sculpture of wood (high relief, polychromed), attributed to John H. Bellamy, catalog no. 55.17, page 116.

Presidential Seal used with permission of The White House, page 119.

Paul Schroeder, back jacket flap.

Contributing Artists

Spencer Lewis and Pat Ortega.

Contributing Writers

Dr. Michael H. Robinson, Director, National Zoo, Washington, D.C.; Dr. Stanwyn G. Shetler, Acting Deputy Director, National Museum of Natural History, Smithsonian Institution; White Deer of Autumn; Richard Cohn; Ken Carey; and Gay Monteverde.